# *Life and Loss:*

## *A Family Confronts Multiple Sclerosis*

By Anthony Browne

Copyright 2017 Michael Brown

All rights reserved.

Published by Blue Dragon Publishing, LLC.

www.blue-dragon-publishing.com

ISBN 978-1-939696-31-1 (paperback)

Library of Congress Control Number: 2017956619

SEL010000 Self-help/Death, Grief, Bereavement

PSY052000 Psychology/Grief and Loss

REL012010 Religion/Christian Life/Death, Grief, Bereavement

Printed in the U.S.A.

 Blue Dragon Publishing

## Table of Contents

Preface ................................................................ 7
Introduction ....................................................... 11

### Part I

A Love Story ....................................................... 17
Who is Toni? ...................................................... 21
Stage One: 1999 ................................................. 29
Stage Two: 2011 ................................................. 36
    Keep Good Records ................................... 40
    Health Care Challenges ............................. 45
    Progression ................................................ 47
Stage Three: 2015 .............................................. 51
    Evolving Situation ..................................... 57
Stage Four: 2016 ................................................ 64
    Next ............................................................ 70

### Part II

What We've Learned ........................................ 75
    Dealing with Grief ..................................... 78
We Pray .............................................................. 82
The Caregiver ..................................................... 88
    Share the Load .......................................... 94
    Who We Are Matters ................................ 98

| | |
|---|---|
| Relying on Trust | 102 |
| Get Help, Any Help | 107 |
| Adjusting Care | 112 |
| Talk About It | 117 |
| Caring for the Caregiver | 121 |
| Feeling Selfish | 125 |
| Final Thoughts | 130 |
| About the Author | 134 |

# *Dedication*

In Loving Memory of Toni.

This story is dedicated by me, Toni's father, to Toni and the family—mom, brother, sister, and son. I leave out their names to protect their privacy, but they know who they are and how important their contributions were. I also dedicate the story to the rest of Toni's huge family—grandparents, aunts and uncles, cousins, brothers-in-law, nieces and nephews.

A special thanks goes to Toni's religious support—Uncle Bobby and Chaplain Collins—and Toni's most special friends who were a part of her life to the end.

Thanks to all of the friends who helped my family make Toni as comfortable as possible throughout this struggle with Multiple Sclerosis. Even if I don't mention you specifically, you know in your heart how Toni felt about you, and you know your efforts were very valuable.

To the Reader, I hope Toni's story helps you in some way.

# *Preface*

I am Toni's father. What you are about to read is a love story about how my family endured my daughter Toni's struggle with Multiple Sclerosis (MS). I will take you through this journey of loving Toni as she fought the disease that attacked her mind and body for 18 years. I will tell you about how we got closer and stronger as a family. I will tell you how we learned about providing care to a loved one…and I will tell you about loss.

Toni passed away from MS in January 2017 after a long illness. She fought as long as she could before going to rest with the Lord.

This recounting of the journey is intended to help you, or maybe someone you know, move through tragedy that requires managing your life and the life of your loved one. There are many ways that the experience can be addressed; this is my way of explaining it to you and making sense of it for my family and me. What I am offering in these pages are my experiences and my recollections of living this unfortunate story.

Living with MS was Toni's cross to bear. She can't tell you this story, so it is my great honor and responsibility to give you the details. I do it to honor Toni and her strength in the struggle. I also write to help my family, and get some closure for myself. It is my hope that telling this story will help you or someone you love.

Toni taught our family so much during her MS journey. Everything that we experienced with her prepared us for the day when we realized that MS was in control. I witnessed Toni routinely fight with MS for some sense of controlling her destiny. At various times, she was strong enough to give us more information about her struggle, helping increase our awareness. At other times, the disease wouldn't allow it. It's amazing how much we didn't know and didn't understand until the end of her life.

The Multiple Sclerosis Foundation estimates the number of effected people in the U.S. at more than 400,000 individuals, with about 200 new cases diagnosed each week. Women tend to be affected more than twice as often as men by this disease. Although MS was discovered in 1868, there is no known cure. Patients may suffer from memory problems, short attention spans, language problems, or organizational difficulties. MS patients may also have cognitive problems and experience pain, tingling, numbness, spasms, fatigue, balance, and dizziness.

We often heard Toni talk about MS, what it meant, and how it affected her. She told us about the importance of setting and reaching goals. She kept very busy raising her son, going to physical therapy, and focusing on getting better. As MS robbed her of her strength and some of her mobility, she continued to hope that these would be small setbacks, and that she could get back to normal.

So, because Toni didn't get to tell the story, I will do it for those she left behind — family, friends, and strangers.

## *Introduction*

Multiple Sclerosis is a disease that attacks the immune system and eats away at the protective covering of a person's nerves. This nerve damage interrupts or distorts the communication between the brain and the body. There are many different symptoms, including ever-present pain, fatigue, vision loss, and impaired coordination. Symptoms may be mitigated and the progression may be slowed with medication; however, this is a progressive disease for which there is no cure.

MS patients may have memory problems, short attention spans, language problems, difficulty staying organized, or some combination of these. You can go to the Multiple Sclerosis Foundation website and read about MS and its effects (https://msfocus.org/).

This book focuses on what my family went through as we supported Toni while she struggled with MS—how our family handled it. I am sharing information on caregiving that I wish we had known at the time.

I'm going to discuss the stages that represent key changes in Toni's life. These stages aren't defined anywhere but in these pages, to help me gather my thoughts in a way that may help you. The stages represent the progression of Toni's disease and how the family learned to cope with caregiving. In each stage, the chapter begins with a summary of what we were going through from the viewpoint of different family members.

Stage One lasts for about 12 years and signals the time when Toni was living a life as-yet unaffected by the MS in an outward, physical way.

It was 1999, and Toni was a vibrant 22-year-old woman enjoying her life. She had early challenges with MS, but she was able to work in a fast-food restaurant and to raise her son on her own. She coached cheerleading and was active in her church. Even as MS began to rob her of the ability to control or balance her body, everyone believed that she was only experiencing a temporary setback that would get better.

We entered Stage Two in 2011, and it lasted about six years. MS started to limit the day-to-day activities that Toni could do comfortably, making it harder for Toni to be self-sufficient and do minor tasks around her apartment that required manual dexterity. She started using a cane and later a walker. She had trouble holding utensils to feed herself.

In 2015, we were faced with new realities of Stage Three as we began to understand the toll MS was taking on Toni. Stage Three was a two-year period when Toni's MS took a turn for the worse. In this stage, she had to use a wheelchair, and she needed assistance with feeding herself because the tremors in her hands were getting worse. After many hospital stays, Toni was moved to a rehabilitation facility.

Fall 2016 brought us to Stage Four and the last six months of Toni's life.

# Part I

# *A Love Story*

I told you this is a love story. It's a story about the love my family gave to my daughter Toni as she fought and struggled with MS. It's a story about how loving Toni and dealing with the disease made our love change over time—growing stronger to support her 18-year battle. It's a story about a love that intensified in ways no one could have imagined at the outset.

My love of Toni compels me to share what I have learned and what I know. That love drives me to offer information that may help some other grieving and desperate family going through similar heartache. It keeps me praying that by recounting Toni's journey, with its highs and lows, I can help someone listen to what is going on, read about what it means, and see what it takes to be supportive of someone affected by MS. This is by no means the only way to view or experience MS with a patient; it is simply my family's journey. And indeed, it was a long and loving journey.

Toni wanted to share her lessons learned with others; that's the kind of person she was. In the beginning, she wanted to write a story to tell others about her experience. She didn't get to do it. She talked often about sharing her knowledge of the disease with others. Unfortunately, she became consumed by the need to make sure that MS did not keep her from reaching goals she set for herself.

Later, as MS robbed her of her strength and mobility, she was busy going to physical therapy. She was busy raising her son. She was busy focusing on getting better. She was busy with the hopes that these would be small setbacks, and she could get back to normal. Maybe it never occurred to her that she would run out of time.

As the MS progressed, Toni still did not write this story. She was dealing with the continued degradation of her motor skills, adapting to life using a walker, and eventually, life in a wheelchair. She was spending time with her son and keeping her spirits high. She was educating the family about the disease and how it was affecting her. Toni was never too busy to be optimistic.

Then MS attacked both Toni's body and memory. She focused with all her might to keep contact with her world. Her strength was now needed for physical therapy. Her resolve was tested during several stays in rehabilitation centers, but she focused on getting well enough to go home. By will and persistence, Toni was able to live at home for several months with her son and her brother. This was a victory for her and for the family. How long she was home did not matter. The important thing was that she achieved another in a series of goals that no one imagined she could achieve.

The family marveled at all the things Toni was able to do. On so many days, sadness was overcome by the love we felt as we watched Toni endure. She was amazing in her efforts to beat MS.

In the late days of her life, she didn't have enough memory or control of her body to tell this story. So, I will try, probably not as successfully as I would like, to tell the story for Toni because MS never allowed her to do it. I write because of the love I have for Toni. I write because I know Toni would want MS patients and their families to know more about this illness. I write because my family experienced a stronger love that any of us imagined, so I want you to know how Toni's family experienced this journey with her.

In the end, Toni gave us so much love, preparing everyone around her for the time when she would go to eternal rest. I offer the experiences that follow to you with the hope that it will prepare others for the reality of loving someone with MS. More than that, I pray this story will help someone who is caring for a loved one who is sick.

I offer you the chance to share with me this love story.

# *Who is Toni?*

I can't tell this story without first making sure that you "know" Toni. I want you to know who she was before the disease came to her—to know the imaginative, freely-loving baby who grew to a girl who grew to a woman. She was clearly the most challenging of my children because she had a great imagination. That imagination sometimes caused joy and grief at the same time.

Toni was born in the fall of 1976, October 5th to be exact, in a military hospital in Goldsboro, North Carolina. Toni was something of a free spirit, so in her honor, I won't give you a chronological trip through her early life. She would be the first to tell you that where you end up is more important than how you got there. She would want you to know that you shouldn't get too wrapped up in the details as long as you get what you need. She would help you free yourself from limitations and regulations, even if it meant that you sometimes got in trouble.

Special right from the start, she had a flare for the unusual, and she didn't crawl at first. She just pulled herself across the floor with her arms. Her mother and I tried to get her to walk instead. She wasn't really interested. In fact, she didn't walk until my father came to visit one summer. He wasn't really into babies and showed no interest in holding her despite being happy to see her; Toni would have none of that. One night she just stood up, walked over to him and climbed into his lap. Toni was extremely mobile and was fascinated by climbing into things—boxes, suitcases, wagons.

As far as talking, we didn't have the chance to marvel at the first word of "Mama" or "Daddy." She didn't talk early, but waited for a road trip. I was in the military working in North Carolina and my mother lived in south New Jersey. The trip home was 10 hours and it was vacation time. Toni said her first words as soon as we set out on the trip, and she didn't stop talking until we got to New Jersey. She never stopped talking and to this day, I don't completely know what she said.

This energetic young lady loved the camera. When she was a toddler, I was trying to become an accomplished photographer. Toni was my subject to help me train on using the camera; she was always ready to have her photo taken. Always. There are far, far more photos of her than my other two children—and she is invariably in their photos. She was so photogenic that she was featured in the military base newspaper hugging Santa one year; a photo that would go viral if taken today. If the camera didn't find her, she found the camera. If she was doing something and someone else was getting their photo taken, she would find a way to get into the action.

Toni was magnetic. Everyone liked Toni. Her laugh was infectious, and she was very open in conversations and relationships. Her openness was so pronounced that she was unable to keep a secret. To her a secret was like a gift, and she wanted to share it. She wanted to give everyone a chance to have the special thrill of knowing the secret. Her desire to make someone else feel good made it virtually impossible for her to keep it to herself. She constantly denied that she couldn't keep a secret. We knew that in Toni's case, no secret could be placed in her hands. We tested her a few times when she was adamant she wouldn't tell, but she failed every time.

As I talk about Toni's inability to keep a secret, I don't want you to think of this as a negative quality. This is the best of her. She couldn't bear to think that she had something of value to another person that she couldn't give them and make them feel better. In her mind, it changed from being a secret to being something that everyone should own and share. It's the only way I can make sense of it.

I'm trying to give you a sense of Toni's concern for others. This is something she inherited from her paternal grandmother. They are so very similar. Her grandmother would truly give you her last dime. They both had the gift of unconditional love and eternal forgiveness. They carried a deeply-cherished faith in God. They both loved to sing and preferred gospel to other kinds of music. They both thought they could save other people, even when they were fighting to save themselves. Neither one of them let their personal plight deter them from caring deeply for others.

Toni had the qualities of her paternal grandmother in that she was always concerned with others. The same way that her grandmother would nurture all of the neighborhood children, Toni would nurture every person she could. And Toni loved to spend time with family. As soon as Toni could talk, she seemed to dedicate herself to gathering the family around her. There was a three-year period when our family lived in New Jersey. Toni's maternal grandparents and paternal grandmother lived within 40 minutes of our home. A visit to the grandparents consisted of part of a day at one home and part of the day at another home. We tried our best to balance the time between the households, but Toni soon tired of this arrangement.

This young lady, not six years old, had a plan. She sat down one day with the grandmothers and suggested that everyone should gather in one house when we visited. That way everyone would be together all the time. She believed that doing it this way would increase the time that we had to visit. Who could argue with this young lady's logic? No one did. She orchestrated her plan to maximize the family time. This example is typical of how much she wanted to bring people together.

Toni didn't play sports until she was 11 or 12 years old. She joined a softball team and quickly became a star. She started in left field and was moved to centerfield when the team needed help at that position. When the team's infield was making a lot of errors, she was moved to shortstop, where she excelled. When the team's third baseman got hurt,

Toni moved to that position. She had a cannon for an arm and was one of the hardest workers on the team. She was a dangerous home-run hitter who had speed on the base paths. Her ability and attitude were rewarded when the team voted for her to be a team captain. She propelled that team to a championship in Germany and was promptly selected for the all-star team.

She brought the same effort, pride, and enthusiasm to cheerleading, which turned out to be her first love. She made the competition squad for cheerleading and her teams won several trophies. She kept cheerleading until she got to high school, when her friends urged her to play softball again. She had many people around her who knew about her softball successes in Germany, and they wanted her to join the team. She gave in, switched back to softball and made the varsity team. Toni played just one year and then returned to cheerleading.

Toni began coaching cheerleading as soon as she graduated from high school. She was great at it. When she graduated, she instituted a traveling team and led her team to victories in several competitions. Along the way, she adopted virtually every girl. At any given point, you would see a big part of the team at our home. It didn't matter whether it was in-season or not; they were there.

Her generosity extended beyond cheerleading. Even after her son was born and she had her own apartment, Toni welcomed anyone and everyone to spend time with her; the young people came from everywhere. Despite having only one child, at 22-years-old, she had many children at any given time. When they saw her anywhere, they flocked to Toni. She was a welcome place to rest and enjoy for her neighborhood; just as Grand mom had been.

At 25, Toni completed an associate's degree program in medical billing at Everest College. To reach this milestone, she purchased a computer, set up a new desk at home, and found ways to use voice recognition software to make her more productive. She had to find a way to keep working and achieving, despite the tremors she had in both hands. She studied diligently and got good grades. By the time she graduated, even being confined to a wheelchair didn't stop her. Toni's joy overflowed on graduation day, and her family could not have been prouder.

Toni let everyone around her experience her wide-eyed aggressiveness about life. She enjoyed so many things. When she was successful, it was a huge success. Even when she failed, she did it in grand style. I believe she captured everything that she could out of life, and then some.

Knowing Toni, you can understand how it was natural for her family to surround her with the love needed to manage her care.

## *Stage One: 1999*

I listened, but I didn't hear.
I read, but I didn't understand.
I saw, but I didn't comprehend.

*A son watched and waited, serving as loving only-child and protector. He championed his mother's cause, making sure she had everything she needed. He kept her needs before his, and he attended to her before going off with his friends.*

*A mother watched and waited, providing whatever support and guidance she could. She was ready to step in and help at any time. Her awareness always keenly pointed toward her daughter. Her decisions ready to be altered—just in case.*

*A brother watched and waited, staying close to help in any way. He stayed connected, mentoring and helping to raise his sister's son, his nephew. At a moment's notice, he was ready for his plans to be changed or surrendered depending on what was needed.*

*A sister watched and waited, keeping in touch from another state. She was always providing moral support and unconditional love. From supportive words to a visit to a check-in, she did what was needed.*

*As her father, I watched and waited. I tried to ease the pressure on her financially and emotionally, adjusting schedules to keep the focus on her and her needs.*

*The rest of the family called to check on Toni. What could we say? "Toni is getting better. Toni is doing well. Toni seems to be getting stronger. Toni is handling this very well." We thought these were the right answers, and maybe at the time, they were. Over time, as we learned the disease, we realized these were not the right answers.*

Now I must tell you the details of Toni's journey with MS so that you can understand the key role caregiving takes in the life of someone with MS or any other debilitating disease. Hopefully you will learn from the experiences my family went through, and it will make your journey easier, although I hope and pray that your situation will end with a more positive outcome.

The day she was diagnosed was like any other. Toni had a young child and was in for a routine checkup. The doctors said that it's common for MS to present itself after childbirth.

It was 1999, and at the time, I listened when 22-year-old Toni was diagnosed with MS. I felt bad for my child, not realizing at this point what it all meant or would mean in the future. I knew that she was a fighter, and I believed that her strength would be the resolution to her sickness. I read briefly about MS, but I missed the part about no cure. I didn't even entertain the notion that this could result in her death. I saw her face and her physical being and thought she looked remarkably well for someone with MS, albeit in the early stages.

My family was optimistic. The optimism came from the hope that the disease was discovered early enough, that good treatment and the advances in medicine would improve things, and that this vibrant young woman would be strong enough to win. Was optimism the correct emotion? No one will ever know; in hindsight, there were things that I needed to know about MS.

Understanding would not have changed what the family went through to help her, or what we deal with now that she is gone, but understanding is important just the same. Sometimes I wish I'd discovered this information before I did. Most times, I wish I didn't understand so well. In those times, I think a lack of knowledge would be so much easier because it might take away the realization that no one could stop the progression of MS. I found myself longing for ignorance. I experienced a selfish desire for this to all be dream where I could just wake up, and it was gone.

I thought that MS could be altered in some way by the medication or by ongoing research. I hoped that MS could be slowed by Toni's mix of medications. There were also days when I realized fully that there was no cure. Each day was a countdown on a timeline that had an unknown end. My family didn't focus on the countdown, just with her life. Yes, sometimes I avoided reality so that I could deal with all that was happening.

MS can cause tremors or uncontrollable shaking. Toni had tremors that ranged from mild to severe and made things very uncomfortable for her. Part of the discomfort was caused by the embarrassment or trepidation she experienced when interacting with others in public.

Toni stayed as strong as she could through all of it. She was winning in the beginning; she really was. She improved her life and that of her son. It was remarkable how she battled the disease, finding small victories along the way. It gave you a warm feeling in your heart to watch her from day-to-day.

Toni was a manager at a fast food chain, taking charge of the operations and conducting training for employees. Her reputation was solid and her good work caught the attention of upper-level management. She was selected to conduct training for people who worked at other locations, ensuring that as many employees as possible had the best chance to succeed. She brought her brother on to help her when she needed a dependable worker. She purchased a new car with her new-found success and moved into a better apartment for her and her son.

This journey with MS is not an easy one, and there are many chances for disappointment. The challenges the MS patient faces are time-consuming, trying, and tough. This was especially true for a single mother raising a son. Toni attacked all of the challenges thrown at her. She went to school events and sporting events any way she could. She lived her life in the best way she knew how.

Most of all, Toni believed. She was so very religious, and her faith kept her going. People around her knew how much faith she put in God, and her church family made sure to come and get her for Sunday services. She went gladly. She sang in the choir and did praise dances during the service to deliver

God's message in a creative way. Toni's church contributions also included coaching a cheerleading team for the church. She did all of this whether using a walker or a wheelchair. And she did all of this without a single complaint.

Toni persevered, taking everyday disappointments as challenges and conquering every one she could. It was amazing how much she could control. She looked life in the eye, and if she asked a question, it was not, "Why me?" The question Toni asked was, "Why *not* me?" Toni studied MS for ways to beat it. She did her homework. She searched for the cure that was still not there. In her own way, in her own world, she searched. Toni took every action that she thought would make the difference. Everyone pitched in to help.

We listened, read, and learned things about the disease. We interacted with experienced professionals without fully comprehending what was really going on.

Mother, father, brother, and sister were right there. We made time to help and stayed in close touch with her. The whole family paid the utmost attention to this fight, even though we didn't know how tough it would become. We were hopeful.

What was really happening to her? She would easily lose her balance and fall from time to time. Early on, she told everyone she was just tired and not being careful. Slowly, the falls became more frequent. Of course, everyone became concerned because she had low-level tremors in her hands, so it was hard for her to catch herself when she lost her balance. We found out later that her balance was affected by the nerve invasiveness of MS. Deep down we knew the disease was getting more aggressive. We didn't know how very aggressive it would become, but we knew it was progressing.

For years, Toni resisted any assistance. Eventually she had to use a cane with a base for better balance. Despite the fact that she didn't like using the cane, it seemed to give her a level of confidence and support. As she got comfortable using it, the family members' level of concern was reduced a bit.

Toni loved to cook and did it very well. One day due to a tremor, she cut herself with the knife. There was anxiety and stitches, but she came through it with the full use of her hand. This was one of the events that signaled the emerging difficulties of suppressing the tremors and being self-sufficient.

## *Stage Two: 2011*

I listened, but I heard only what I
wanted to hear.
I read, but I understood only what I
needed to understand.
I saw, but I didn't connect with all
possibilities.

*A son watched and waited, meticulously taking care of his mother and shielding her from anything that made her journey harder. He worked endlessly between healthcare and school, giving up time for homework, sports, and even friends to be available for his mom. He was constantly there with the love she needed.*

*A mother watched and waited, providing counseling as well as care. The mental part of the disease was showing itself in the form of lost memory and even something akin to hallucinations. Her mother focused on providing loving care, offering words of wisdom as well as the physical assistance wherever it was needed. She made decisions, altered them, abandoned them, and made new ones to make sure she was always giving the best of what was available, the best of what she had to give.*

*A brother watched and waited, adjusting his schedule to put her first every day in every way. He connected with her on a more personal and spiritual level than maybe he realized. His relationship with Toni's son, his nephew, grew, moving effortlessly between uncle and nephew, friend and partner, big and little brother, and connected souls. This interchange was obvious to the whole family, and it was beautiful.*

*A sister watched and waited, making the endless, long phone calls to stay in touch. This gave her a piece of "being in the room" as much as she could. She provided love, tough love, and unconditional love in equal amounts. It seemed that she always knew exactly what "kind" of love was needed and when it had to be delivered. Her support was ever-present and she never took a day off. She gave every minute of love she had to give, and then she gave more.*

*Her father watched and waited, trying to be the glue that holds it all together. Easing the financial burden can have a profound effect on the journey. Seeking creative ways to address medical bills and the expenses that grew beyond Toni's budget was time consuming but worth it. It became clear that dollars that were spent in times past without any thought should now be redirected to health care and living expenses. It wasn't hard. Go out to dinner one less time.*

*Postpone getting that new "item" that you really don't need. There was more joy in giving that money to Toni's care than the fleeting enjoyment of a restaurant meal or a new shirt. This was easy.*

*The rest of the family called to check on Toni. What could we say? We talked of her progress with optimism to give them information without the burden we faced daily. We didn't want to give them more information than they needed. We would tell them more if they came to visit. We knew that you couldn't really know how she was doing unless you spent time in her presence. At this point, we didn't know the right answers. We just wanted to do the right thing in communicating Toni's status. As we learned more about the disease, we were not sure about the answers.*

At age 35, Toni was still working, still driving, and still taking care of her son. Even with her struggles, Toni was promoted to manager at the fast-food restaurant. She supervised the other employees, took care of opening and closing, and made the bank deposits at the end of the day. Even as she was moving up in her career, MS was gaining ground, but we were all still optimistic that things would get better. Toni led that optimism, convinced that she could get all the way back to where she was when she was first diagnosed with MS.

As the disease began to affect her more, she had a series of falls. She visited the doctor and would then report back to the family. I listened to the reports and felt that the falls were unfortunate, but not overly serious. What I "heard" was that an adjustment to her medications would help. The words I "heard" were that she was back on the road to recovery. I knew all about her strong will and winning spirit, and believed that her strength would put her back on the road to finding a resolution to the disease.

With those incomplete and misguided conclusions, I didn't read any more about MS. I still didn't make a connection between no cure and the notion that this could result in her death. I saw Toni's face and her physical being and thought that, even though she had some falls, she was finding a path to a better way of dealing with the disease. I was right and wrong. Toni was being strong and finding ways to cope, but MS was gaining ground. We didn't even know the rate of increase of the progression; we could just feel it happening.

# Keep Good Records

During this stage, my family was asked lots of questions about Toni's medical history. The doctors wanted to know when was she diagnosed, the date of her last appointment, and what were her medications. Most of the time, she could answer for herself. As the disease progressed and robbed her of her memory, her son became the most important source of information. Even at a young age, he was there step-by-step, and he has a mind like a steel trap. He provided details, copies, and even passwords at times. We learned how important history of the disease was for doctors to recreate the progression to determine the next possible steps.

We tried to help the medical teams with Toni's history, but we didn't have all of the information. You see, Toni took care most of her own medical issues and financial information for a very long time. Once her mind became affected by the MS, she didn't have command of all the answers to our questions.

We didn't know the timeframes for when she changed medicines, about experimental procedures that had been discussed with her, or about the requirements for her next doctor's appointment. We only knew when she was diagnosed and how long she lived with the disease. As her son grew up, he was able to provide a lot of information, but he was still young and couldn't be expected to answer everything.

It was hard to fill in the history when the medical teams needed it. The doctors and nurses wanted to build a history to do research on her condition to arrive at possible approaches to treatment. Toni's records were in multiple places in various formats. Some were on the computer, some on random strips of paper, some in opened or unopened mail, and some in personal notes in a filing cabinet. There were large gaps in the records before we started around-the-clock care.

The recordkeeping is hard enough with one doctor. Toni had several doctors to take care of the different issues of MS—medications, eyes, physical therapy, etc. These doctors and their staffs had records on Toni that had no common source where we could access them.

The family came to the realization that we needed to keep our own set of records for her, so we collected past appointments and any notes, test results, prescriptions, etc. We were not aware at this point that there are apps and online services available to help you collect and share information among doctors and other family members. Some examples of this are iBlueButton, Track My Medical Records, Capzule PHR, and My Medical. Use of this kind of app would have helped us keep everyone on the same page.

Having a one-stop shop on medical history is invaluable. We could have provided sleep schedules, over-the-counter medications, or physical therapy habits to assist in the medical efforts. We now know that we have a federally guaranteed right to see and get copies of our medical records. People are owed this information from their health plan administrators, doctors, hospitals, pharmacies, and extended care facilities, so be sure you pursue this angle. You may have to pay for copies of the information because some health care sources charge a few cents per page after a certain page limit. You can minimize or eliminate this cost if the records are available electronically. If you can only get the records in a paper copy, take the time to scan and save them in a safe location.

In fact, medical records and history intensified in their importance in Stages Three and Four that you will read about later. We only had a complete record of her medical struggles from October 2015 on because we were constantly there with her during this time. We knew about the many hospital visits, 911 calls to come to the apartment, and emergency room visits—but we couldn't fully recreate her history.

Once Toni's memory started failing, it was even harder for her to participate in providing the historical background on her care.

We didn't realize how significant the issue was until one particular doctor's visit. We thought this was a new doctor for Toni, so were surprised to find out she had treated her in 2011. The doctor knew some of the Toni's history, and didn't think the timeline Toni was providing was the correct chronology. She helped us collect more of Toni's medical history.

We now understand that collecting and managing medical history is a valuable tool in dealing with your loved one. Keep a binder or a shared computer folder that families who need access can read. Organize chronologically and note any major changes in the patient's status or medications. Record emergency room visits and hospitalizations. If you have access to a patient portal for the records, be sure to download what you can for your personal storage. Many companies have developed programs to help you manage medical history by requesting access to new records from doctors and listing all diagnoses, symptoms, and medications. Some of these programs feature shared access between you and the involved doctors.

Take the time to do recordkeeping. Include information like medications, surgeries, known allergies, and pre-existing conditions. Write a summary after every doctor's visit. Don't forget blood pressure, weight, and cholesterol. MS patients often have vision problems, so it's important to include vision tests.

Keep a vital information datasheet handy. If something happens to you and you can't be there, this will offer important information for the person taking your place in giving care or in getting the patient admitted to the emergency room. Give all caregivers a copy, then put a copy in an overnight bag for the patient. You can even keep a copy in your wallet or car. The information should include the patient's primary care physician contact information, the preferred hospital in case of an emergency room visit, any known allergies, and any conditions or special needs that first responders need to be aware of. Be prepared with an organized medical history, and everyone will have a sense of comfort that they can navigate any emergency.

# Health Care Challenges

The challenge of health care is availability, affordability, and regulations all wrapped into one. There was care Toni could afford but couldn't meet the necessary qualifications to receive. There was care that she was qualified to get but couldn't afford. There was care that was affordable and available, and there was even a waiver for some of this care that took care of the cost. However, in some cases, getting the waiver and not paying for the care translated to income and that created a problem with how much overall care she was entitled to get. You always have to be careful not to exceed the patient's entitlement. If your income goes up, your fair share of the health care cost does as well.

The medical challenges seem endless and insurmountable at times. Many times, the family could navigate all of the requirements for getting medical coverage or special equipment only to find that it was not possible to receive the benefits based on state or federal regulations for care. In the long run, what that meant to the family was that much of Toni's care came through the emergency room.

We had to "wait" for her to get sick enough to warrant an ambulance coming to transport her to the emergency room. Once there, the emergent issues were fully covered—well, almost. There were some bills from the emergency room that went beyond her medical plan or that took time to get paid and went delinquent. These emergency room visits gave her doctor a chance to see if the current mix of medications was right for her current care.

This emergency-room scenario played out many times. Once when she was very sick and got admitted to the hospital, it presented an opportunity to get another opinion on her care. The family had been concerned that her doctor may not have considered alternative treatments because her condition seemed to be degrading. Toni was not improving even though this was a great doctor who she was very happy with. MS families tend to be in tune with new treatments and experiments because we are always searching for answers. Everyone delivering care wanted to see improvement. Yes, selfishly, we wanted to see improvement. Lovingly, we *needed* to see improvement.

On this particular occasion, Toni's doctor was not readily available. The emergency room medical crew believed there was a better approach to Toni's care in terms of the combination of medications.

The lead doctor made some changes. Toni stayed in the hospital for a few weeks and started to improve, to get stronger. When she was released, she was under the care of a new doctor. Things were getting better, and the family was encouraged.

## Progression

When the MS progressed to the point that Toni couldn't work at the restaurant, she continued to manage restaurant shifts and scheduling from home. People were counting on her, and she wasn't going to let them down.

Then she finally reached a point where she could no longer work. She had been a great restaurant manager for a very long time—a job she had to give it up when she was placed on Social Security medical disability. Even part-time work would have exceeded the amount she could make while receiving disability payments from the government—one more obstacle Toni had to navigate as she battled the disease.

The family remained committed to working together to address all challenges. Her eyesight got a worse. She was becoming weaker and the risk of falling became a problem; when she lost her balance, she couldn't catch her body. She was at risk for concussions because a few times her head hit the ground in a fall.

She had several emergency room visits and several hospital-stays during this stage of her MS journey. Toni helped us understand that she had new concerns about how the MS was affecting her, and this was challenging her positive attitude about recovery.

The family also heard the concerns of doctors and nurses about the severity and number of the lesions on Toni's brain. I read more about MS, and Toni explained to me about how she felt and what MS was doing to her. I could now understand the amazingly uphill fight she was undertaking. I realized how monumental dealing with Toni's MS would continue to be. I comprehended that this was a fight for today, tomorrow, and really, always. I knew that this was a fight that the whole family had to join to make her life as comfortable as it could be.

I knew her strength was still there, and she was fully engaged in finding a resolution; however, now I saw what I never wanted to see. I struggled with wild thoughts of how bad MS could get, but I never considered death as an option. I saw her face and her physical being and realized her determination and resolve to work on her own quality of life. We would engage as a family and do what we needed to do. MS was becoming stronger and harder for Toni to resist.

There was an incident when Toni was in a car accident. Her body wouldn't let her touch the correct pedal. I remember going to get her from the scene of the accident. When I arrived, I saw that she wasn't hurt; she was distraught and crying. She said, "Dad, I really messed up!"

There was so much hurt in her voice. I didn't understand it at the time. Now, I think it was one of the first times in her life that she was entertaining the possibility of weakness. The first time she allowed the notion that the limitations and difficulties in managing her life might be beyond her control.

Soon after that, Toni started using a walker sometimes and was then given a motorized scooter to help her move around. She avoided getting in a wheelchair. I think she believed that going to a wheelchair was accepting that she would not walk again on her own. She persevered with the walker. She got around better than I could imagine.

A few months later, she got sick again. Another episode sent her to the emergency room. Toni experienced a temporary inability to speak and eat. This relapse seemed to come over her suddenly.

Toni's next challenge was a short stay in a rehabilitation facility. We went through several weeks of the hospital trying to get her in a rehabilitation facility, and we were faced with a new set of problems.

The first issue was that the first facility where they tried to send her did not accept her insurance. The second issue had to do with her age. Toni was 38 years old, and two of the facilities that did take her insurance were set up for senior citizens. Toni was too young to get help from this facility that had the care she needed; it was a facility for senior citizens. Finally, the family found a facility where she could be admitted. What a relief!

In the next stage, I will take you through the move to the rehabilitation facility and the escalation of Toni's MS.

## *Stage Three: 2015*

I listened, and I heard.
I read, and I understood.
I saw, and I comprehended.

*A son took action, helping to get the rental house ready for his mom. He got his mom's permission and tried to enter the military before he turned 18, because he wanted to take her as his dependent for health care reasons. He was still focused on whatever she needed.*

*A mother took action. She was the primary reason the family found the rental place. She set things up for her daughter and evaluated what Toni needed. When there was a setback in terms of what insurance would pay for, she made up the difference. She was the rock!*

*A brother took action to move all of the furniture into the house, and then began to work out housing costs and feeding schedules. He adjusted his work schedule to give him the maximum time in the house with his sister. He never tired of searching for the next answer to her needs.*

*A sister took action to research financial matters. She worked to inform creditors of her sister's situation and to find ways to reduce or mitigate any debt. She researched every avenue to find a better way to get care or an outlet to help with costs of care.*

*Her father took action to help set up the house. This role was fluid and required moving from moral support for Toni and family members to working on financial assistance to addressing gaps in medical coverage that might be resolved.*

*Now when the family called to check on Toni, we simply said that she was very sick.*

Things were good in early 2015, but challenges soon came. In the previous stage, Toni's condition took a turn for the worse, and we simply couldn't care for her at home. We needed to admit her to a rehabilitation facility.

Because of day-to-day events in life, the family was not able to spend as much time as we usually did when Toni was in the hospital. We believed that the staff at the rehabilitation facility would take over for much of the time we couldn't be there. We were wrong.

At this point, Toni couldn't speak well, and the attendants at the facility had to help her eat. We learned over time that the staff at the facility seemed to be in a transition period. One day Toni got plenty of help; the next, she sat in her bed for hours with no attention at all.

When we realized the limitations on the staff's time, we resurrected our more aggressive care schedule so we could go to the facility more often to be with Toni. The family provided the care facility with everyone's primary and alternate contact information. That meant when we got a call, whoever was closest hurried to the facility to provide whatever was needed.

The situation was exacerbated by Toni's belief that the staff was trying to hurt her. We now know that these thoughts were a result of the invasiveness of MS on her brain activity.

There were still days when we would come and no nurse had been to see her all day; she hadn't bathed, eaten, or taken her latest dose of medication. Toni got sick again before our family could complain about treatment conditions. This time was a more severe relapse. She lost all speech and wasn't eating, so the facility staff and the on-site doctor tried to reach her regular doctor. As they ran many tests and tried to figure out what was going on with her, she got worse. I ended up half-convincing, half-begging the on-call neurologist to admit her back to the hospital.

This time, when we joined her in the emergency room, she seemed to be in a coma. We couldn't understand the few utterances she could make. She had to be fed intravenously. These were dark days. The doctors didn't know what brought on this episode. The family was getting used to this answer and to the uncertainty that came with it. MS is unpredictable in the way it affects the body and mind. That unpredictability was upsetting Toni's world once again.

Day became night and night became day as we took turns sitting with her in the hospital. The routine changed for all of us. For me, it was rise in the morning and pack an overnight bag with something to eat. I had to plan as if I wouldn't be coming home for days. Then, as I worked, I coordinated with the family to determine who would see Toni on the "day shift" and who would take the interim visit until the "night crew" could arrive. Typically, any family that was in town would gather at the hospital room. We watched her favorite shows: Steve Harvey, Judge Judy, and the Celebrity Name Game. And we always played gospel music for her.

This hospital visit was quite another experience. A new doctor came to evaluate Toni this time. His news was not good. I was at the hospital with my brother when the doctor told me, "This could be her new baseline. We just don't know."

My heart sunk, and my knees got weak. I'm grateful that my older brother was there with me; I couldn't have survived this day without him. Telling the family of this news was devastating—again. Toni had recovered from these episodes many times, although this time might be different. Several days went by, and she still was not talking or feeding herself. Seeing her this way with feeding tubes devastated the family yet again. We couldn't comprehend the thought that we might not see the kind of recoveries that we had experienced before.

We wept with her and for her. The saving grace at this point was that it didn't seem that Toni realized how sick she was. She came out of the coma, but the hallucinations were back, and she was experiencing feelings that someone on the staff was trying to harm her. She wouldn't let people help her, wouldn't eat.

This only changed when her mother came to the hospital. Her mom spent extra time there and refused to leave until Toni was set for the night. Her mother also started going in the morning to make sure each day started well. The staff helped, and things got a little better.

Each day was filled with another round of tests as the doctors tried to figure out what was wrong. The doctors said they were amazed at how many lesions she had on her brain; they said they rarely see that many in someone so young (under 40).

Eventually Toni made enough progress to be transferred from the hospital to a rehabilitation facility. It was a different facility than the first time, but she still didn't want to be here. She felt this was giving in to the possibility that she wouldn't get better. For her, this was not a step in a positive direction. The family, however, worked to convince her that this was a good thing. She was getting aggressive physical therapy and interacting with other people instead of just lying in a hospital bed. She let us know every day that she wasn't happy to be in a rehab center.

The people were nice, and she had made some very good friends. Even with this, she wanted to go back to her apartment. She was once again the youngest patient, and it bothered her to make friends only to lose them to recovery or death. Death was often the reason, and that took a toll on Toni. She worried aloud that she might meet the same fate. Still, her resolve was strong most of the time. She decided that if she could get better and leave the rehabilitation facility, there would be no talk of dying.

Unfortunately, she had been sick for so long that the family had broken her lease and moved her belongings out of the apartment and into storage. We knew she couldn't go back there because she needed a handicap-accessible living situation.

## Evolving Situation

Toni had been in the rehabilitation center since Halloween of 2014. The search for living accommodations was ongoing, and holidays and special events took on even more importance. Toni was having success with physical therapy, and she set a goal to attend her son's high school graduation. She worked tirelessly to be ready to attend, and she made it!

In June 2015, the family hired a nurse to help get Toni to the graduation; she was on the floor of the graduation hall when her son walked across the stage. We had a family dinner and stayed the night in a hotel near the graduation site. The family, once again, gathered around to make Toni's journey easier.

Late in Stage Three, the family started planning for what would happen when Toni was well enough to leave the rehabilitation facility and come home. My home was not handicapped-accessible, so the family was looking at assisted living and handicapped-accessible solutions.

As we headed into 2016, days turned into weeks. The family plan was to move Toni, her son, and her brother into an apartment together. Her brother would be the primary caregiver. This would be a bonus because it ensured that we always had an adult available to handle any emergency. Toni's son was only 17 but continued to keep up with her care. He was juggled college while trying to spend as much time with his mother as he could.

The search for a handicapped-accessible apartment in our part of Virginia was difficult. We never found the three-bedroom apartment we needed. All of the handicapped-accessible apartments we checked out had one or two limitations. What we experienced was that either the third bedroom was not a full bedroom or the place had no storage. Two places we went to had given up storage to allow an open floor plan conducive to moving a wheelchair around. Regardless, on Toni's behalf, the family applied for and failed to secure several different places.

The family took a welcome break from house hunting in July 2016, when her son turned 18. The rehabilitation facility where Toni resided at that time provided a private room for a birthday celebration, complete with presents and food. You could see the pride on Toni's face as we celebrated the special day. Like the old days, her son sat on her lap and gave her a big kiss. This was a much-needed celebration.

Finally, in September 2016, the family secured a lease on a three-bedroom house. This was a perfect solution, and the family started to set up the house for Toni to come home. The landlord was gracious, agreeing that the family could make handicapped-accessible adjustments or renovations within reason by getting his prior permission. The first thing added was a ramp for front-door access. More preparations were needed, like adding a lock-box for caregiver access and planning to widen the master bathroom door. A friend of Toni's donated a hospital bed for her.

It was a big day when the family got the word that Toni would be discharged soon. The family had a care plan and a home that we thought would be a long-term solution. We hoped this arrangement would last for years, and we set out to make sure that Toni's health care solution considered all participants.

So now caregiving was more important than ever. In that effort, it was crucial that the family members who were engaged in Toni's health care could take care of their own health and welfare at the same time that they helped her.

In October 2016, the family set up Toni's 40th birthday party in the facility. The staff provided a private room, and everyone gathered to celebrate Toni's special day. She was happy and doing well. She was getting stronger through physical therapy, and her thoughts turned to getting home. This was a heartwarming and uplifting celebration that provided a break from the challenges and the difficulty of dealing with MS.

Despite the fact that the family was hesitant to do big celebrations like these, we found that we needed them as much as Toni did. These celebrations were a relief to the stress of the situation.

What I know now is that the challenges of dealing with holidays can be gifts in the form of blessings. For instance, we spent Christmas 2015 and 2016 in the hospital with Toni and her MS. We tried to be as cheerful as we could for Toni's sake.

On Christmas Day 2015 we decorated the room and took presents to celebrate the day. Toni couldn't enjoy them very much, but she had an awareness of the presents, and it was fine. She had been depressed about being in the hospital and perked up when the whole family was together for the special day. It was an amazing day. She was in and out of consciousness with a general awareness of all of us in the room. She was fast to respond to the sound of her brother's voice and slow to respond to other things.

She kept asking about the whereabouts of her son until he arrived, and then she cried. She laughed and cried on and off as her son reminisced out loud about their lives together and told his usual jokes. Without warning, she would ask for her sister, mom, or dad; seemingly as a way to let us know that she was aware of our presence and able to participate in the conversations. At different times, she would blurt out something that happened to us as a family in the past. This gave us a great sense that she still had mental strength left.

Toni spent Christmas Day 2016 in the hospital as well; this time with the loss of the ability to speak clearly. We brought her a holiday blanket, didn't decorate the room or bring presents. Toni didn't have the awareness at this point to know about or enjoy the presents, in our collective opinion. The happiness of the day really came from the fact that her new pastor was present to conduct a Christmas service for Toni, helping to make this a joyous occasion.

Deeply religious, Toni nodded her head in response to the church service. At times, you could even hear humming as she tried to sing along with the hymns. After several hours, Toni took some medication, and we let her rest. We went home, and everyone opened their presents with Toni's still nestled beneath the family tree. This bittersweet day was beautiful because we understood that the church service brought joy to Toni. These are the kinds of gifts that keep on giving.

The greater gift from spending holidays this way was the focus on how a person *feels* about Christmas Day, rather than what they *get* from the day. This ordeal tells me that we don't think enough about the impact of the holiday season on a person. We should be thankful for being together instead of for the money we spent on each other. My family can't take credit for being extremely wise in arriving at this realization. We just came to realize, all at the same time, that our actions were the real holiday gifts, and the time we spent with Toni was priceless. Learning how to cope with MS and endure Toni's battle with MS was our gift to a person in need. Toni led us to these realizations through her strength and her faith.

The family was happy that we had found a good way to handle holidays and special events. Now that we had moved past the holidays, it was time to make yet another adjustment in the way we cared for Toni. Her needs had changed again.

## *Stage Four: 2016*

I listened;
I read;
I saw her at peace.

*A son watched and waited in prayer.*
*A mother watched and waited in prayer.*
*A brother watched and waited in prayer.*
*A sister watched and waited in prayer.*
*A father watched and waited in prayer.*

Debilitating sickness. More emergency room trips. Several hospitals stays. A severe relapse and Toni lost her ability to speak. She was back in the hospital. The whole family prayed for the best possible outcome. Several times Toni lost her memory. Thank goodness these things were not permanent.

Toni did have one "blind spot" from 2015. She was in the hospital from Halloween 2015 until January 2016, a timeframe she just couldn't remember. The family tried unsuccessfully to bring this back to her memory. In fact, Toni reacted with disbelief about the severity of her condition during hospitalization. This was frustrating because it was a period when she was the sickest since she was diagnosed. But maybe it was for the best.

Day-by-day she struggled mightily. The doctors said the lesions on her brain, one of the signs of the progression of the disease, were increasing. Then she would fight and come out of it. Then she would get sick again.

The doctors said the lesions were the worst they'd ever seen. The family was now unfortunately familiar with the disease, and we understood that it was progressing; we just didn't know how much. Toni knew it was serious, but she couldn't always tell the family about it. We could see it.

After she had been in the rehabilitation center for almost a year, she insisted she wanted to go home; we did everything we could to make it happen. The family did whatever was necessary and more because Toni's strength was failing her and her memory was in and out. I could see the daily changes—some good, some bad—that were altering her being and her life.

Near the end of Toni's days, she experienced something called a true relapse, which is when spinal cord and brain nerves get swollen or irritated. According to explanations from the MS Foundation, the nerves lose myelin or the coating that surrounds and protects them. They are replaced by a plaque that alters the electrical signals moving up and down the nerves. This can mean that the signals get slower, that they get distorted, or maybe that they stop. A typical example is optic neuritis, the inflammation that affects the signal between the brain and the eye, causing the patient's loss of sight.

A true relapse exacerbation is also called an attack or flare-up, and symptoms vary from person to person. Some are characterized by only one symptom, such as inflammation in an area of the central nervous system, while others may affect more than one area. These occurrences last from a few days to several weeks or months and may be treated with an increased dose of steroids under a doctor's inpatient or outpatient care (paraphrasing from National MS Society website). When the relapse is over, the patient may or may not continue to feel the effects.

Because of her struggle, we know that there are different types of MS that may vary in the manner and the severity of how they affect a patient. In Toni's case, the flare-ups could be major or minor, lasting a few days, several weeks, or months. However long they may have been, they severely affected Toni's day-to-day quality of life.

In Stage Four, she needed help with virtually everything. She was confined to a wheelchair and needed some help with eating because the tremors made it impossible to hold a spoon or a fork.

Her face was still lovely, even though she was clearly not herself. In fact, the family didn't know how much she was not herself until the neurologist told us she was not responding to any treatments, experimental or conventional. I saw her face and her physical being, and realized that, in addition to being in constant pain, she was tired. She was tired of this journey. She was not giving up, because she still paid attention to raising her teenage son and did all she could do for him. Her strength came and went.

I didn't want to face reality. Deep down in my soul I felt all the ways the disease was robbing her of the benefits of life. Toni's next stop was intensive care. They did all they could for her. More tests and more experimental treatments brought no real change. That is when the lead doctor called the family together into what felt like the smallest room I've ever been in. As we listened to the latest update, it got smaller.

The doctor told us that they had tried everything, and that while Toni was not getting worse, she was not responding. She couldn't tell us what was going on, and she just stared into space. There was minimal movement in her limbs. The doctor told us they didn't know what else to do, and that we had to make a decision.

We had been prepared a few weeks earlier. Specialists from the hospital, including a nurse assigned to our family, told us that there would come a time when we might only be able to make Toni comfortable. The family made the choice at that time that she would not be resuscitated if she stopped breathing.

In that small room, the doctor said that they were virtually out of options. The specialists who had come in to try experimental treatments had tried everything. They were no longer on the case. There was nothing else for them to do.

The doctor then gave us two options. First, we could try life-sustaining operations to keep Toni alive and see if she would recover over time. The doctor told us that he didn't believe this would happen. She had been unresponsive too long.

Option one required at least two surgeries, and her brother and sister were clear that Toni was afraid of surgery. Her son agreed with that assessment.

The second option was to make her as comfortable as possible and see how that worked out. The family knew this meant that this option could end her life. Toni had not spoken to us or had anything to eat on her own for days. We were again devastated.

We didn't want to make this selection. The family wanted Toni to survive, but we knew how tired she was. The family stopped focusing so much on ourselves, and did what Toni would want. No more poking with needles, no more hospital straps, no more lab visits.

As hard as it was to face, deep down we all knew it was time to see her at peace. We all slowly and painfully came to the same realization at different times in the continuum of care. As we sat with the medical team one last time, we made the difficult decision to let her rest. It was time to let her go with the Lord.

The hospital moved her to a more private room with low lights. A few days later, her vitals were still strong, and we were still taking our turns visiting Toni. In fact, many days the whole family gathered in the room talking about Toni's life. The family still believes to this day she could hear us and that she was responding spiritually. The pastor was almost always there.

On January 16, 2017, we left the hospital to get dinner. Her brother said he would visit later that night. As we had dinner, her brother called to say, "Toni took her last breath. She's gone."

The world stopped for me. I was not ready. The family was not ready. We knew the call would come at some point. On the day it came, we were not ready.

This was the most pain I've felt in my life. When we got to the hospital we hugged each other. We kissed Toni. We cried. We kissed Toni again. This was truly the lowest point in my life.

Toni was a highly religious person and loved to go to church and worship. I sang the first two verses of a very special church song for her. "The Old Rugged Cross" is a beautiful song written in 1912 by George Bennard, a coal miner turned Salvation Army worker turned pastor.

She now slept peacefully; our angel was on her way to heaven. As Toni went to the Lord, there was no more pain.

## Next

After an eternity passed in one night, the family started the notifications to immediate family that Toni was gone. We told them, "She is not in pain."

Finally, for the first time in more than 18 years of Toni's life, she was not in pain. As a family, we rejoice about that every minute of every day.

Some wonderful things happened in the time of enormous loss. These were things we needed, even though we didn't know it at the time. Toni's uncle, a deacon in his out-of-town church, served as mentor, friend, counselor, and pastor. Toni's pastor came and stayed for hours on end. He had spent the night with Toni on a couple of occasions to give the family some time to sleep and eat. Now he was spending time with us.

The whole family was hurting. When I spoke at the wake, I said, "Right now, I want you to close your eyes, and when you close your eyes, Toni will come to you. She will come to you as she comes to me. She will come and she will kiss you on the cheek and say everything is all right. And then she'll sleep again."

This is the memory of Toni that my family has. This is the memory we need to have. We focus on the idea that any time we are grieving over her loss, we can close our eyes and the memory of Toni will come to us. I see her come to me so very many nights, always when I need comforting.

*Part II*

## *What We've Learned*

You've heard Toni's story. Now I want to tell you what we—the family—learned from it, so perhaps it will help you through your own personal journey.

As I watched this story unfold and went through various experiences of the family providing Toni's support, I had no awareness of the overall lessons I would learn. As I recount what I learned now, I realize just how much Toni had to deal with. Even in that realization, I admit I probably know very little of what she actually experienced. I also realize how very much Toni taught my family and me during this process. I guess she was taking care of us.

Still, in looking back I know I learned to pay attention to life. In the early days, you hope that the news is not as bad as it seems. You hope that everything will turn out all right. You go through days, weeks, and months without thinking what this means. You avoid thoughts about whether the MS will get worse. You believe—you MUST believe—that this will be a remarkable case of remission. You suppose that they may even find a cure. This is what you must do.

What I learned is that this is the time to pay special attention to everything going on around you. Changes are happening to someone you love. They are coming slowly. Toni's body was changing and her consciousness was being altered. Of course, some of these changes were too gradual to notice. Keep in mind that if you don't live with your loved one on a daily basis, the changes are harder to see. They go through things and experience high and lows that change them in many ways, and, since they can't always tell you what is happening or what happened, you have to be attentive and flexible to provide the best care possible.

I want you to know that as your loved one discusses their plight, you may not be able to get the full meaning. You can understand what you hear, and you can have sympathy, but I don't believe you can fully comprehend it all. You can't really put yourself in their shoes, and you certainly can't feel what they're feeling. This is tough, because when it's your child, you want to take the pain away and carry it for them. You can't.

You can only give your love and support. Your loved one is in pain and she's fighting to maintain her intelligence and consciousness. Toni told us many of these things to help us with the reality of MS. There's so much you can't possibly know about; the guilt you feel if you are upset with the patient, the sheer exhaustion of needing to always pay attention to MS, the frustration of finding a solution for care that fails, or the unfairness of MS affecting your loved one. Also, you still have the thought that this will improve, that she will get better.

What I can guarantee is that you will be challenged. There will be things you don't want to know. There will be things you can't understand. I urge you to stay close to your loved one and do the best you can with whatever you learn and whatever you need to do to support them. When they have several good days, or weeks, or months in a row, you'll want to breathe a sigh of relief. And you should.

What I know now is that you have to understand that MS is still there. I hope the experience and the outcome is different than what my family faced. Even if that is the case, with MS, you have to be prepared that it could get worse. You have to realize that the progression of MS can speed up or slow down without any warning. This can be a bumpy road or a roller coaster. You just don't know. Try to keep your wits about you and be strong for your loved one and for yourself.

The times supporting Toni were very interesting. We enjoyed the time we spent helping Toni and we were exhausted; just drained. The toll MS would take on our loved one and the family still has not been revealed. In fact, my family is still learning the full impact of MS to this day. Each member was profoundly affected.

## Dealing with Grief

As I move through my days, I wonder how I will continue to cope with this grief—this loss. People all around me wonder what I'm going through. Some ask how it's going, and some don't. A good friend asked me the other day, "How do I help you? What do I say to you? When do I say it? What if I don't know what to say?"

I realized I didn't know the answers. I didn't know them for Toni. I don't know them for myself. My friend's questions forced me to examine this part of my grieving process.

I have come to know that I benefit from concentric circles of people who move in and out of my life and keep me going. They all help in their own way and all of them are needed.

It begins with immediate family who are there every day, feeling everything I feel almost at the exact moment that I feel it. They know my pain even if I don't say I'm in pain. They see my highs and lows, and they understand.

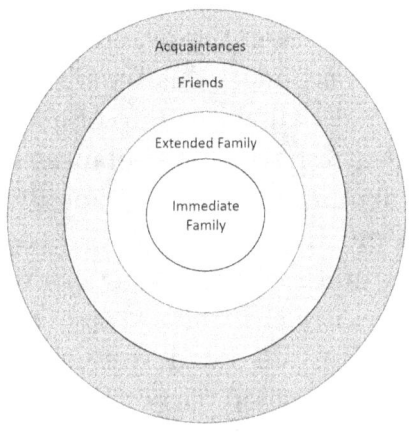

My extended family is remarkable. I have many people who check on me to find out how I'm coping. They'll stop by when they're around. They send me words of wisdom or a nice photo that improves my day. These are the people I can lean on when my immediate family is unavailable or when I need to give my immediate family a break from my issues. This has been more valuable than I can express during the grieving process.

Next are the friends in my life who enrich my days. Their contributions are just as important even though we talk less frequently than any of my family groups. I actually benefit from the fact that I can ignore them at times. If I don't feel like talking or I don't know how to respond to their question, I can just ignore it. I can't always do that with family, and I appreciate that I can disconnect this way if I want to. This is a very valuable group of people.

Finally, I have acquaintances. I don't give them much information, and they don't give me much information. They care, and they contribute to my grieving process when we communicate. I don't know when or if they will help me, but I appreciate having them as even a small part of my journey.

You will get all kinds of advice from many well-meaning people on how to deal with your grief. Just remember, it's your grief. Remind yourself that it's okay to mourn and to take as much time as you need. There is no timetable, and the events of your life will signal the progression of your grief.

One way to deal with your grief is to face it head-on. That's why I'm writing this book. I'm telling the story that Toni couldn't tell to memorialize her strength and her struggle.

Some may recommend you take down notes to capture things as they occur to make sure you don't forget them. That's not what my family did. First, we didn't have time to take notes or make a diary. And second, we didn't know or wouldn't accept that this was a battle that would end in Toni's death. We didn't consider this. We couldn't. We just lived the days to make them as good as they could be. Period.

I thought that we would have to build a memorial on holidays and special days in honor of Toni's memory. In reality, it was not necessary. From her passing in January to Mother's Day, daily memories served to honor her. So many times, we thought about her or we were forced back to a moment in time when a special thing happened. *That* is our memorial to Toni. So, while creating traditions on special days is the right thing for some to do, it wasn't necessary in our family. The rhythm of everyday life continues to put the memory of Toni and all the special things she did—before and after her illness—vividly and constantly in front of us. We are blessed by the wonderful times we had, despite the unfortunate effects of MS.

# *We Pray*

I have very definite ways in which I deal with my grief. I call my approach **WE PRAY** and I offer it to those around me to help with the way we interact as I deal with my grief. These are ways to cope and manage life despite this great loss.

> **WE PRAY**
> **W**ait
> **E**mbrace
> **P**repare
> **R**emember
> **A**ccept
> **Y**esterday

I came up with this collection of words deliberately to remind me of how religious my daughter was. She loved the church and craved gospel music. **WE PRAY** helps me personally focus on the thoughts and feelings relating to Toni.

When I say *Wait*, I'm talking about understanding that I must find my own time to cope. *Embrace* is learning that my happiness is as important as my grief. *Prepare* is the knowledge that there are days coming that will automatically challenge me. Many say that birthdays and the date of death are the two key dates; I won't argue this point. I will always **Remember** what happened, and it's important to face those memories. Of course, I keep Toni in mind even when it's painful. As I grieve for her, I must *Accept* that, in addition to finding time to cope, I must continue to find my own way to grieve. I accept that it's fine that my way may not fit what other people think is correct. I can't change *Yesterday*, but I can make today and tomorrow better. Talking with people about my loss can be painful and therapeutic at the same time.

So now I offer this same tool while looking at it from a different angle. I think this way of focusing can aid family and friends who want to, or must, deal with disease and loss. What follows is a deeper explanation of **WE PRAY** to assist when talking about or experiencing someone else's personal situation.

**WAIT**: This loss challenges how one views the world and the importance that is placed on every day of your life. It teaches you about grief and recovery. Remember that when you are talking to someone in my situation, nothing you can say will cause more grief than what I'm already experiencing. That means that if you have a question or a heartfelt thought, I ask that you please share it with me. It might just make my day. I hope you will be enriched by standing with me or spending time as I endure one of the most difficult times that anyone can experience. Your presence and attention is appreciated.

**EMBRACE**: Walk with me as I come to understand and embrace that my happiness and my grief are equally important. I embrace my family, giving them my time and attention, as they give me the opportunity to lose it emotionally at any time I need to. Strength in love and friendship can be medicinal for my journey. It's important to embrace our feelings and accept them. And it's important for others to give us time to do that.

**PREPARE**: I do agree that Toni's birthday and the day of her passing are key dates that will always tug at my heart. As those special dates draw closer, you have to prepare yourself. Some fantasize about what their loved one would be like today if they were still with us. Some create rituals or recount their loved one's arrival in this world. Some prefer to be alone with the thoughts of that special person and what he or she meant to them. Time is the only thing that will help me figure out how I will continue to approach my loss. These special days, and the days leading up to them and the days that follow them, bring great emotion. As you listen to me talk about Toni, I may or may not share with you what's happening inside my heart. I guarantee you will know that I am dealing with my grief. I might need some space, so if I seem distant at these times, I am sorry. It's part of the grieving process.

**REMEMBER**: You can't grasp what we're going through unless you've gone through it yourself, and even then, your experience was probably very different—or will be. Your discomfort may keep you from approaching me. Please understand that I also have discomfort about your approach, but it's important that we both work past that discomfort to communicate. I want you to remember Toni, if even for a moment. You can tell me what you remember, and I hope you will feel good about listening when I do the same with you. Whether or not you knew Toni, please ask me about her and don't worry about the awkwardness. There is joy in the telling! It makes me—and my family—smile inside and out. We are proud of Toni and who she was.

**ACCEPT**: I am devastated by the loss of my first-born child, and this will not go away. The feelings of pain and loss, stronger some days and weaker on others, are always there! My life and my family's lives will never be the same. We will get through it and keep on living for Toni's sake. We have to believe that this is what she would have wanted for us. Your support is greatly appreciated, and I know you want to help me, especially if you are a close friend. Please don't try to help me figure out when it's time to move forward and get back to my life. That is my domain only. The best you can do for me is to recognize what I'm going through, observe how I deal with it, and accept that you can't help me more than you already have. Make no mistake—by paying attention, you help me. Don't worry, that is the most that you can truly give me. I have to go the rest of the way on my own.

**YESTERDAY**: Know that I struggle to honor my late daughter and her time on this earth, and that it's an ongoing battle of pain and regret for outliving your child. Sometimes I feel guilty that I am now enjoying things in life (like pleasure travel) that I wouldn't consider when she was alive. I remember longing for the time when she might be well enough to enjoy them again. Unfortunately, that time never came. The grieving process requires that I balance happiness and sadness and do the best that I can every day. I also have to live for my other children and for my grandson, and that would make Toni very happy.

# *The Caregiver*

A caregiver must listen to hear what's important to their patient; must read the signs and understand what is happening; and must take responsibility for the quality of each day in the patient's life.

Providing care really is a state of mind where people commit to providing something that is difficult to find or pay for. You can take care of someone as an action, but *providing care* is a huge responsibility that can bring great joy and enormous stress—sometimes at the same time. Those who provide care are partners with the patient in dealing with the daily ups and downs of MS. It can be broken down into caregiving and caretaking.

A caretaker is someone employed to take care of a person. A caregiver is one who voluntarily cares for an individual who needs assistance. Both are special kinds of people. As my family experienced the battle with Toni's MS, we lived through the challenges of *caregiving*.

Caretakers are hired to do things for someone that they can't do themselves. They also complete tasks that the patient elects not to do, despite having the ability to do them. Because caretakers are basically obligated to provide care, they may find it easier to take charge rather than to work closely with the patient to ensure the patient is maintaining as much independence as possible. If they aren't careful, this situation could lead the caretaker to become fully responsible for the patient's behavior and choices without their input.

This is an important distinction, because my family worked hard to carry out Toni's wishes for her care as much as we could. We didn't want to end up as caretakers who were obligated and needed to be compensated for care.

My family was more concerned that we might not be able or qualified to deliver the valuable kind of medical care we knew Toni deserved. We weren't trained in this field, but we made up for it with our loving attention.

We were caregivers who worked to find harmony between Toni's feelings and our feelings about care. We had to pay attention to each person's strengths and weaknesses to ensure that we set goals and carried out plans. This was our way to ensure that we didn't lose our patience and sanity in the process. You do things for your loved one because they can't do it for themselves, and because you want to help them pursue a day in the future when they might be able to handle things on their own. Care is a gift you give the patient.

This felt right and allowed us to spend time with Toni that was loving, reenergizing, and inspiring. We worked to honor Toni's requests and help her make choices for the way her care would proceed. When she couldn't determine the best choice of action on her own, the family worked on a cooperative approach to guide the decision. For instance, when Toni was having trouble walking, she didn't want to choose the wheelchair option. We worked with her to get a cane with a large base and then helped her transition to a walker.

We took an empathetic approach with Toni and stressed positive messages and hope for her recovery. We had our hard times and our doubts, but we were careful not to share those with her. We did, of course, work to give her the truth about her situation at every opportunity. This was important because of the way MS affected her thought processes and memory.

We worked to determine long-term solutions as we concentrated day-to-day on only taking action on the things Toni requested of us. We tailored our approach to her abilities and emotional endurance.

It's important to know that giving care rarely gets easier without around-the-clock professional help. There were days when Toni would cry uncontrollably and be especially irritable, and our attempts to console her failed. This was MS at work, but we didn't always know that. It was even worse when she had a bad day and I had mine.

There were times when I couldn't even get out of bed and get moving. I knew we had to give care that day but, after days on end that looked the same, I needed sleep that didn't include an alarm clock. Even when I was finally awake, I felt a kind of temporary paralysis where I couldn't get myself to go where I needed to be and to do the things I needed to do. I simply couldn't move at that moment.

I had a long talk with a nationally-certified counselor who is licensed in Texas and Florida, and she helped me find a deeper understanding of the challenges of continuing the caregiver role. The conversation helped me think about what to do when I was stuck and felt that I couldn't go another inch to provide care.

The counselor told me that in these times of challenge, the weight of the caregiver's responsibility is so great that professional counseling is needed. My family didn't feel we had the time to seek professional help of this type, though we did take advantage of any specialist at the hospital who reached out to us as part of patient services.

There was an angel of a nurse who spent time with us while Toni was in the hospital. We never suspected these were some of Toni's last days on earth until the nurse began talking with us. She was the one who was in the room with us when we were told the doctors could no longer help Toni; the disease had gone too far. This angel was important because, at this point, we needed care more than Toni did.

Even before this final prognosis, we had great challenges. There were several times when Toni believed that the people giving her a shot were trying to kill her. The counselor explained that there was a "war zone" going on in Toni's brain and causing this dilemma. We got through these times by staying in tune with Toni's daily routines.

Redirecting her attention to fast-forward through these episodes helped her to reset her day. Simply playing a recording of her favorite show or a movie she liked, or turning on her favorite music app helped to move her to another place emotionally—kind of like tricking her to think it was another day so she could start over on a different path.

The bottom line of caregiving, I found, is that you must focus on helping the patient exhibit their normal behaviors in the most familiar settings at the usual times. You must do this as much as possible to allow the patient to live their old routine. Familiarity seems to help. Despite the constant challenges, you will feel happy and rewarded when you have even the smallest of successes.

Good caregiving means finding harmony between your patient's feelings and your feelings. You must understand your strengths and weaknesses so you can provide the best care without losing yourself in the process. Your interaction with the patient also requires that you come to grips with your negative emotions and your ability to adapt to unexpected challenges. A clear focus on the goal of your efforts is a great path to success.

My family's goal was simple: we wanted to keep Toni as comfortable as possible, take care of her unpaid financial issues, and allow her to live at home instead of a public healthcare facility. To make this a reality, we had to start with a schedule that everyone understood. We needed to be a cohesive team, and we needed to cover for each other so that we could minimize gaps and issues in providing Toni's care.

## Share the Load

Keep in mind that care should be a family undertaking. Caregiving is best handled when everyone tries to understand that, while everyone wants basically the same outcome, their ability to participate may differ. Try to make everyone comfortable by understanding other points of view on providing care. Avoid judging another person's motivations or actions and just accept that they are doing their best in their own way.

We all have our own strengths. When Toni could no longer get into the bathroom by herself, she needed help from her mother. Her mom diligently ensured that health care needs and handicapped-accessible opportunities were identified and satisfied. She offered words of wisdom and helping Toni remember things.

Her brother normally had the difficult task—mentally and physically—of helping to pick Toni up and move her around so she could be cleaned and dressed for bed. He continued to adjust his schedule to be constantly available to give care and helped with raising his nephew. I couldn't have done it as much as he did. He is a saint!

Toni's son was both child and protector, championing her cause at every opportunity. He was always at her side helping and doing whatever he could to make things better. He worked to ease the journey by juggling his schoolwork and helping with her health care. Even at that young age, he gave up time for homework, sports, and friends to be available for his mom. He continuously made sure no one did anything to upset her journey. He was her rock.

Toni's sister lived in another state and provided ongoing moral support and, later, financial management assistance. She researched every avenue to find a better way to get care or an outlet to help with the costs of care.

As her father, I strived to ease any financial burden on Toni while managing overall family and care schedules to make sure everything was synchronized. I worked to make sure everyone on the team was fed and rested while I searched for alternative treatments and support groups.

It's helpful to establish a home rhythm for giving care so that everyone can be on the same page. Our family's routine was to check in the morning before work to make sure Toni had what she needed and that the daytime nurse had arrived. Then we had assigned roles of going to the house to take care of dinner and anything else that was needed. After dinner, Toni had certain programs she liked, so we had a few hours break to do any personal things that needed attention. When possible, we worked, did homework, or watched our own favorite shows at the shared home where Toni was living. Then we completed a sort of family checklist to make her comfortable for the night before we all went off to bed.

With all of these new challenges, this new approach served us well. It made it easier to flex when someone needed to take personal time for a few hours or a few days. We supported each other in this.

We combined honesty, understanding, patience, and forgiveness to deliver our love and provide the best care we could. We did it as a team. We had challenges that required our physical and mental togetherness. We also benefited from humor; it really is good medicine. Laughter can provide increased energy by easing the stress of a setback or challenge. It eases tensions and helps to bond relationships stronger than they ever were before.

We learned to cope with so many things. The family handled stress by growing and learning about the crisis and by loving the patient and the members of our family. If you find yourself in this kind of situation, try to be happy that you are providing something that can't be provided any other way. You'll find the hidden strength to deal with everything that comes your way.

Seek out the positive in every situation and emphasize that aspect. Change the issue from a negative to a positive and move forward. This will bring you comfort and rejuvenation. A positive approach helps you manage the situation.

You'll need to recognize and accept the times when you need to reach out for help. An outside person or another point of view can put things in perspective, or show them in a different light. That outside help ensures that the family can keep care manageable at all times. Be flexible when giving care so you can work through crises by bending, changing, and/or adapting to whatever comes your way. You'll be a stronger family because of it.

One thing that you will need to do when caring for your loved one is to forget—at least temporarily. Some equate this to meditation. The burden of care weighs heavily on your mind. You'll probably spend a lot of time wondering whether you could have done something differently, could have done something better, or did something correctly. These are valid concerns, and forgetting or meditating can help each family member and caregiver with their need to regenerate their mind and body. Some would say the body is easy because rest or exercise puts you back on the path. The mind is different.

You will continue to figure things out and then second guess yourself over and over. What you need is a time out. Take time to decompress and rejuvenate. As bad as it sounds, you need short departures to clear your mind. This means go to a movie, eat a leisurely dinner, go shopping, or just relax. It's hard, but you must do this. You need strength and mental wellness to provide the kind of care you deem important.

## Who We Are Matters

When giving care, it's helpful to pay attention to gender differences between the patient and the care provider, especially if they are siblings.

Despite the fact that we all face the same challenges based on the responsibility of care, men and women tend to have different experiences. There are countless studies demonstrating that men tend to have a harder time expressing what they feel and may be more likely than women to suppress those feelings or their emotional reactions. Men have been known to be slow to ask for help and don't always use the resources that are available to caregivers.

These same studies show that women are great at accessing supportive networks and being able to express their feelings freely. Women, on average, tend to miss participating in outside activities and managing their own health. MS Society literature reports that women report more physical and emotional ailments than do male caregivers. On the other hand, when giving care, men are more likely to manage their own health better than women are.

While the patient's needs are the *primary* concern, the bottom line is that quality of care is really all about the family or the caregiver. If you push yourself too hard or expect too much of yourself, that can cause problems. You have to be willing to accept that you are doing the best you can when you can.

I say this because I see caregiving as both a curse and a gift.

It's a curse because it can sap your strength and wreak havoc with the rhythm of your life. It's a curse because the challenges you face in providing care can be summed up with two words: pressure and expectation.

Pressure comes from everywhere. The pressure to perform and give your loved one everything he or she needs in every waking moment. The pressure of maintaining the routine work schedules and responsibilities that you have as you provide this care. You have to work, and there are things you need to do to take care of your mental and physical well-being. If you get sick, you must go to the doctor, so you should avoid getting sick so you can continue care. I see that as great pressure.

Expectation refers to an anticipated outcome. You want the care you give to be the right amount given the right way—but it's hard. You may not have the training. For instance, you need to be trained on the transfer of the patient from bed to toilet or bed to wheelchair or wheelchair to car. You should be trained on administering shots. The expectation from your loved one, the patient, is that you can and will do those things successfully. You want to be great at giving care, although it can be frustrating and embarrassing, as well as mentally and physically draining. There is also the expectation you may feel from those around you who are watching how you care for her and thinking you will have it under control. They don't know, and they don't see, the trying times in most cases. These are real issues with which you will have to deal.

I said caregiving is also a gift.

There is a gift each and every day you do it. It's a gift when you do it well based on the happiness and comfort it brings to the patient. There is a gift when it does not go well, but knowing that you gave all you had to make it right. There is still a gift in knowing you will be back tomorrow to do it all again.

For my family, there was the satisfaction we all received because we were bringing whatever resources, ability, and energy we could muster to take care of Toni.

Families and caregivers simply find a way to handle the bad and the good to be successful. That's why giving care is as much about the provider as it is about the patient. You have some negative and positive things to deal with, and you need to find a balance in those things so that you can handle everything. If you focus on your reasons for providing care, you can find that balance. That balance is what keeps you going and sustains you when things are tough.

# Relying on Trust

We relied on trust between family members to allow us to provide the best care possible. Trust is knowing that someone will provide the care when you can't, even if you don't ask them to. Trust is knowing that if you oversleep someone on the "team" will wake up in time to provide care. That trust allowed our family to provide quality, coordinated care.

And we did it as a cohesive team. After taking everyone's comments and availability into account, we arrived at shared values, interests, and responsibilities.

The shared values were pretty easy to agree on because we all wanted what was best for Toni. We wanted her to make her own decisions for as long as possible to the extent she could make those decisions. Toni needed to remain in charge of every aspect of her life that she was able to.

The family agreed that pursuing a rental house was in Toni's best interest. We decided it was the best possible living situation because it gave Toni some independence while allowing for handicapped adjustments.

The family shared responsibilities by creating a schedule so that everyone knew what was expected of them and when they were projected to give care or pick up supplies. We agreed to work together to resolve schedule conflicts.

Trusting each other made our caregiving efforts consistent and effective. Each member of the family and extended family had the occasion to sacrifice their own wants and desires to allow others' interests or needs to prevail for the good of the overall effort. We worked hard to be fair to the interests of everyone as we tried to make each issue or concern a win-win for all involved. Compromise was considered in every family-sanctioned action. We used our collective resources to complete our caregiving.

There were still times when the family had to relinquish control to an outside agency for care. That was also acceptable.

As we carefully crafted approaches to healthcare and made necessary adjustments, the family made sure that we collaborated on everything. The family also tried to make the decided course of action more of a suggestion than a direct order. That gave people the flexibility to adjust in their own way and still accomplish the overall goal.

We openly discussed what was at stake and outlined the overall care situation we wanted to achieve. We analyzed options, and each person acted as a safety net for others. When things went wrong, for whatever reason, we didn't place blame. We just worked through the difficulty so we could keep moving ahead.

My family discovered the true meaning and value of trust during our caregiving journey. To build and nurture it, everyone needed to believe that they would benefit from the caregiving enterprise in some way. That belief seemed to fuel their continued commitment. Family members found that the more they believed in the approach we agreed upon, the more active they could be and the more they wanted to help. This was a challenging commitment to make day-in and day-out that resulted from love and strengthened the trust between us. Our trusting relationship was nurtured by the realization that Toni was getting something of value—loving care.

The most effective caregiving happens when people adjust the interactions to find common ground between the patient's needs and the caregiver's personal needs. These adjustments can take the caregiving from a clinical relationship to one of emotional attachment.

Trust between Toni and her caregivers was also an important consideration, especially for those who were not in her family. It helps if each party to the caregiving knows and accepts what the other party is doing or thinking.

A good technique for caregivers is learning the nonverbal mannerisms of the patient to allow anticipation of her needs. The family knew things were working well when Toni and the caregiver in question acted as partners. They grew to know each other and found a personal connection and ease of communication that helped the trusting relationship. The growing relationship gained strength, and it was easy to see that there was mutual respect.

It was rewarding to have so many people working toward what was best for Toni.

We had a family relationship that became unbelievably stronger through providing care to Toni. We also strengthened relationships with our extended family. There were people who we knew and trusted, and we were able to connect with them and enlist their help in our overall care plan. They were an invaluable part of the support we provided for Toni.

Each person was ultimately engaged in seeking value and in sharing that value with others. The shared effort was treasured and made our interactions powerful and memorable. Everyone was open to exchanges where constructive ideas and opinions were shared. We enjoyed the active roles and joint responsibility that everyone signed up to that resulted in quality time with our loved one.

The interaction then moved to one of protection, where both parties enjoyed time together and their experience transcended a working relationship. In the case of most of the non-family caregivers who worked with Toni, this was more like two friends getting together. When it was really good, the relationship became a solid connection. They made decisions together and found themselves in unplanned activities. There was now real security in the relationship.

The trust we shared was imperative when an emergency arose. The caregiving relationship requires an immediate trust as you realize that the severity of the current need and the nature of the injury or illness creates a situation where the patient is in a position where she has no choice but to trust those working to save her or make her more comfortable.

Some experts refer to this part of the caregiving interaction as the essential relationship, and it is a time when immediate trust is necessary to allow administration of aggressive or painful care.

This relationship lasts as long as is needed to survive the invasive treatment or crisis.

When the MS was most active and caused Toni to get very ill, she responded easily to family members. If dealing with extended family she didn't see as often, or with non-related caregivers, she might not have the same level of trust when needed.

# Get Help, Any Help

There's a lot to learn in terms of providing care. It's important to do your homework and pay attention to every hospital visit and care experience. I say this because you can learn a lot from the great professionals in hospitals, emergency rooms, and rehabilitation centers who do a wonderful job. You have to get help from wherever you can find it.

Family care responsibilities can range from a few functional challenges, to learning how to give injections, to supporting a medical team. At the critical stages of dealing with MS, you participate in—or are the sole provider for—toileting, dressing, moving, medicating, and feeding. The medical care from insurance only goes so far, and it doesn't always cover the patient 24-hours a day. It must be supplemented. We were always ready and willing to help even if we were not always capable of providing the kind of help needed.

I can't tell you how it will or won't work for you. I will say that you can't get discouraged, especially because there can be so many challenges with medical care costs. We dealt with annual payment limits and cost sharing rules. When she had an MS episode that could not be covered by her insurance, or when she couldn't get in to see her physician, we had to use the emergency room. In fact, it became a regular and necessary part of her care. This is just a fact of life, because we couldn't afford to wait when the MS was most active. She needed to be tested in a timely manner to determine what the issue was. That meant regular CAT scans to assess the status of the lesions on her brain.

Toni was able to get experimental drugs that were either paid by insurance or donated because of the research value. There were still limitations, and limitations often meant missing payments and rising debt.

Another challenge is that if the family members help by paying after the patient has reached her annual limit of medical coverage, those additional funds can be counted as income and can have an adverse effect on the patient's tax standing. It's important to contact your insurance entity to understand how expenditures from someone other than the patient can affect the coverage plan. We watched this carefully and covered what we could. Unfortunately, it was never enough to cover the bills. In dealing with MS, you will find yourself in a constant battle to get and protect medical coverage.

One blessing was that the supplemental medical training given to care providers is very often free. The injections come in a variety of forms, and someone from the doctor's office or the hospital trained us to give them. The lifting can be challenging, even if you're strong. If the patient can help you, it's easier to lift them and move them from bed to wheelchair to toilet, etc. However, if the patient can't help, they become heavier than their body weight. There was training from the rehabilitation centers to demonstrate how to do it correctly to avoid injuring yourself or the patient.

Yes, there is training, methodologies, and aids to help with all of this, but this too can come with many challenges. For instance, Toni's insurance provided a mechanical lift that was perfect for Toni, only it had no seat. Technicians at Toni's rehabilitation facility showed us how to use towels and blankets as a makeshift seat for the lift. These methods, while less than perfectly functional, were better than nothing. No one could ever find a seat for us. We did our own quest and, after searching various companies for three months, we found that the seat had been discontinued. The family adapted to make the best of the situation while the company searched for another model that was "complete," but we never received a replacement.

Another important part of care is getting help wherever you can find it. Participating with support groups online or in person is something highly recommended in all literature of the National Multiple Sclerosis Society (nationalmssociety.org). These groups have people who have something in common with you; the participants have gone through what you are facing, or they are currently facing the same kind of care issues. They may be able to provide moral support and advice to include legal and financial tips.

Make sure you talk with your supervisor and your employer about what you're going through. Everyone likes their privacy. Providing the basics of your situation makes that midnight call to say, "I don't know when I'll be in to work," so much easier. Most employers understand and are flexible in these situations if they know what's going on. They might even offer work from home or flexible schedules to improve your ability to provide care. Check the conditions of your health care plan at work to see if there are provisions for caring for a family member.

Identify programs that are available to your loved one, figure them out, determine who to call, and take advantage of every benefit. I'm talking about Medicaid, Medicare, disability payments, Veterans Administration benefits, and any other support you can think of. You may even be able to find reduced-price or free meals to reduce grocery costs for the family.

Don't get discouraged if your loved one doesn't qualify for some of these benefits and don't give up when the answers are slow in coming or doors are closing when you try to access care or support. In this case, persistence is your friend.

Work with the doctor and the hospital's medical team to try to find affordable treatment strategies. Providing health care is expensive, regardless of your financial situation. Hospitals now have specialists who can cut through the red tape and help get assistive devices like walkers, wheelchairs, or canes.

It's a good idea to open communications with pharmaceutical companies, if you can. The medications for MS tend to be very expensive, so talk with drug companies and do research to find programs for qualifying families that provide low-cost prescription drugs. The patient's doctor, clinic, or hospital can help connect you with sales representatives, in some cases.

There are respite care programs that can give caregivers a much-needed break at just the right time. These are programs that provide short-term caregivers so that the primary person responsible can take a break. Your health insurance may cover all or part of this cost. You can create your own respite answer by coordinating with family and friends to get them to visit for a few hours, days, or weeks.

## Adjusting Care

As we found ways to improve Toni's care, it was important to adjust our caregiving style to fit Toni's particular situation, one that changed over time. Caregivers must be educated on the specifics of the effects of MS, so they can relate to what the patient is going through. MS is a complicated disease, and the family did a lot of reading and discussing with the medical team to understand the reasons for certain medical approaches and medication combinations.

Early in her fight with MS, Toni had command of this information. In the later stages, we had to become knowledgeable so we could help her continue to understand what was happening to her. We worked very hard to provide these medical facts in layman's terms so they were useful and understandable. We also followed up after Toni's appointments to get updates, pick up medications, get testing results, and then explain all of this to her.

As far as caregiving style, I've done a lot of reading about how you approach and spend time with the patient. For instance, some experts say that caregivers who sit instead of stand when communicating to the patient might seem more friendly or competent. You can search and find any number of fascinating articles on caregiving that offer tips like allowing periods of silence to be beneficial to care. Doing this gives the patient "space" when they are thoughtful or introspective. Caregivers should also make sure they don't interrupt the patient when they are speaking and encourage discussions over question-and-answer sessions.

I feel that the *content* of what you communicate about just as important as the *style*. It's important to allow the patient to bring the experiences of their life into the care situation. Whatever Toni remembered or discussed about events of her life, we made sure to never make a judgement about how those events were instrumental (or not) in her current medical situation. Care is about now, and we felt that trying to link to the past in search of a reason would not be beneficial for anyone concerned. We did, however, freely discuss any mistakes or missteps in Toni's care to make sure she knew that we were human beings doing the best we could. We assured her that any actions we took in providing her care could be adjusted or discontinued if she did not feel they were right for her. That is, of course, unless the action we took was a medical activity directed by her team of doctors.

Our delivery of caregiving paid attention to content and style. The family helped Toni accept the reasons for medical approaches and medication combinations. The family worked diligently to follow up after appointments to secure updates, acquire medications, and find testing results. I believe we did a good job of providing care for Toni. I just wish we had the benefit of some of the suggestions mentioned here.

We also had to be compassionate so Toni could maintain a sense of herself. Our ability to have effective communications throughout Toni's care allowed us to include her thoughts, feelings, and challenges in her care.

We remained sensitive to the need for her to take control of her situation as much as possible. Her individualism was an important part of her care, and it was necessary as we worked to achieve shared consensus in caregiving.

We worked together to cope with Toni's MS and its effect on her. The family wanted to be realistic as we participated in her efforts to find a cure for her MS. Our collective hope for the future was often shared with her. We discussed how she wanted to improve, and she focused on reducing her pain. This was an excellent goal because it speaks to one that she could achieve—if even for a day. Regardless of what was happening at any time, we made sure she knew that we would always be with her, and that we would provide whatever was necessary for her care and comfort.

The family accepted the daily challenge of making the adjustments a reality. We made sure Toni was part of the discussions about her continued care, and even though there were times when she could not communicate clearly, we gave her decisions priority in the care plan. We focused on reducing her pain, improving her comfort, and finding little victories in things she could do on her own. She took comfort in working the TV remote control. When the tremors became too bad for her to hold it, the local cable company provided a voice-activated remote.

We paid attention to what she was doing or thinking, and we created caring partnerships, not patient-caretaker commitments. We made sure that the care that was given worked for all parties concerned. We stressed safety and security and allowed friendships that were beyond family ties to flourish. Decisions were made together, and there was a true sense of urgency when there was an emergency. We tried to mitigate the situation when the needed care was aggressive or painful. This allowed Toni to do what was necessary to get through the invasive treatment or crisis.

Compassion allowed us to be sensitive to her needs and allowed her to take charge of her own situation. We stressed a realistic approach that fostered hope for the future and the motivation to keep trying to get better.

# Talk About It

If you are a family member serving as a caregiver, take your time with your grief and know that there is no right or wrong way to go through this. It's also important to understand that everyone grieves in their own way and at their own time, so don't try to impose your expectations on others. Stay in close touch with family and manage one day at a time.

I know it's hard, but try to talk about your child with your loved ones and with other people. It's difficult for friends or acquaintances to know what to do or say. They're trying to avoid causing or increasing your pain. You're the only one who can tell them what's important to you and what this grieving period means. Be up front, and let them know when you don't want to talk, or when you can't.

Many people will tell you, "If you need anything or you need to talk, let me know." Take this with a grain of salt. In my experience, this is something people are conditioned to say as the "right thing" when someone dies. They don't always think about what they are really offering. And they don't think about the commitment they're making. They're saying they will be there for you when you need them. I hope you have a strong family support structure to get you through these times, because the offer of help or a listening ear may never be realized from those that mean well.

When we lost Toni, I had people say these very things to me. I dismissed them at first because I have a strong family and extended family support structure. However, soon after her death, I needed to talk to someone outside of my family. Please don't misunderstand; I could and did talk to my family. I just wanted them to have a break from this kind of discussion.

I reached out to a few people who said they would be there for me. Luckily, one of them *was* there. That person took the time to talk with me, and more importantly, to listen. A second person brought dinner on a day when I couldn't even work out a way to go through a drive-through for fast food. That's the good news.

At least two people did not come through for me. I understand this is hard on everyone. In fact, one person promised to call me back and never did. The other person never acknowledged my note asking to speak with him. I recount these stories as a way of helping people understand what these offers mean to the grieving.

Offers of help are only valuable if you are truly ready to stop what you're doing and be the answer to the grieving person's need. While it's hard for a person to know what to say or do in these unfortunate times, it is even harder for a person who is grieving to extend themselves to seek assistance, advice, or a shoulder to cry on. It's hard because each time you reach out, there is the potential that you have to tell the story all over again. There is the potential that you will get a question that you haven't thought of, forcing you to come up with the answer. There is the potential that discussing the situation out loud touches a nerve that sends you right back to the darkest hour of grief. So, I urge family and friends who want to help: choose your words carefully. Above all else, make sure that you will be willing to do what you've offered to do. You could be the key to improving the day for a grieving person.

One of the hardest things to do, even now, is to talk about your child. You go through a period when you can't—or won't—talk about them in the past tense. It seems that this helps give you some additional time to adjust to the fact that they're no longer here. Talking about your deceased loved one carries you through the wake, the burial, and the long days and difficult nights that will follow. If you're like me, you will go through a period when you jump between past and present tense in talking about your loved one. This was a juggling act where I was trying to determine the best way to make my point.

If I was discussing Toni with my family, it seemed natural to talk in the past tense. There were so many different memories where someone would say that she loved that show, or she loved that song, or she loved that event.

If I was telling someone about her loss it seemed, for the most part, that I did it in present tense to let them know about the end: what we saw, what we felt, and how she was finally at rest. I also talked about how we would honor her and what our plans would be as a family.

If I was talking to someone about her and they didn't know she had been sick, or if they hadn't seen her in many years, I tended to move between past and present tense. This was the best way to characterize what happened and when it happened.

Now, I mostly discuss her in past tense. Some of the family still cannot talk about her in the past tense, or at all. This is fine; as I said earlier, you need to let everyone grieve in their own way.

# Caring for the Caregiver

As we moved through the MS journey with Toni, we were desperately searching for the resources to make it work, striving to find something to make it easier. Toni's needs were our primary concern; however, the bottom line was that quality of care is really all about the family or the caregiver. Caregivers have some negative and positive things to deal with, and being able to find a balance between these is necessary to handle the challenges.

Dealing with MS becomes a partnership. The family comes together to provide whatever is necessary. Having a family willing and able to make sacrifices to provide care is important to success. The effort can be overwhelming at times and having others with you is always helpful.

The National Multiple Sclerosis Society is a great resource for caregivers. The society urges you to get involved in self-help groups that can give you an outlet for your emotions and can provide information on all matters of care.

The society shares information about affiliated self-help groups from across the country and suggests that spiritual and religious organizations are good places to find support and guidance. There are even online caregiver chat groups for those caregivers who need to stay close to their loved one and find it harder to go to meetings.

Some caregivers are known to feel invisible because it seems that everyone's attention is on the patient, and no one understands the daily challenges they face in delivering care. People don't tend to ask how the caregiver is doing; the focus is solely on the patient.

Another thing that can affect caregivers are their own feelings of disloyalty. For instance, if I'm too tired to help today or I have an appointment of my own, I might feel that I'm letting my loved one down. Some feel they are being selfish by taking care of themselves. This is far from the truth, but something that people genuinely feel.

I know from experience that the caregiver's mental and physical well-being is vital, because you want to be at your best when caring for your loved one. If you have these feelings of invisibility or disloyalty, try to understand that these feelings are normal, and they happen to a lot of people who are doing what you do. Accept them as normal, and you will be able to deal with them.

You need to take care of yourself. Rest as much as you can and make sure to eat three meals a day as often as you can. You might find it useful to read about parental bereavement or to join a support group. I found it helpful to read even more about MS and how it affects a person. Each bit of information helped me understand some of the issues and gave context to some of the events that I remembered so vividly. For instance, when Toni had trouble speaking, I could connect that to the activity of lesions on the brain and how they affected the nerves. When she had trouble with her vision, I could understand that as one of the ways MS affects the patient.

Next, as much as you want to take care of your loved one, you need some outside activities. Understand that when you're providing care, you are totally focused, and you will tend to block out everything else in your world. Still, the world does indeed go on. You must find a way to live outside of giving care so you can regenerate. It's easy to feel trapped in this responsibility, even when you voluntarily entered into this arrangement. You may feel out of touch with personal and social relationships because your days are filled with healthcare. You may feel you don't have the time, or you can't sacrifice the time, for your interests and activities.

It is understandable to feel this way; however, I urge you to fight it every now and then. We had a nurse we could hire from time-to-time to give us a break. This allowed family members to have a night or a weekend off. It also allowed Toni to have a new companion who was closer to her age. Everyone involved got a break to decompress.

This leads to another significant issue for caregivers: communication. The best thing about my family's approach to helping Toni care for herself was that we had excellent two-way communication. We were able to discuss our fears openly and get moral support from each other. As we learned more about the disease and how to care for Toni, we started working on long-term plans and goals to build a sense of security about what we were doing and how we were doing it.

The family was always working toward a comprehensive care plan. Unpredictability is a concern, so the plan covered a lot of things. We had to consider how to build in extra travel time and have a backup ride available, just in case. When she had an appointment or we wanted to take her out, we found that we needed to call ahead or drive by to determine accessibility of entrances, exits, and bathroom facilities. We made a conscious effort to discuss dinner plans by the noon hour each day. This helped with awareness when we might be spending the night in the emergency room. We had to know operating hours for food establishments to ensure we ate something.

We had to make a sleeping plan, taking turns getting to bed for a few hours during those long stays in the emergency room or hospital. Our family plan also included a list of people who could provide assistance or support in emergencies. Some of these would provide services, and some would just be moral support.

Of course, the *primary* focus is not on the caregiver. The patient takes center stage in this real-life drama and what's important is what needs to be done for the good of the patient. Still, there are serious issues that could arise and hinder the family's continuing ability and mindset in terms of providing care. These issues can range from confusion about the disease, to dependency, to isolation, to anger. Everyone must deal with these issues so that they don't become pent up frustrations. The consequences of those feelings could make a tough situation tougher.

## Feeling Selfish

I still feel bad that I had selfish feelings when Toni had long visits to the emergency room or long stays in the hospital. I loved her (still do!) with all my heart, yet the waiting was unbearable at times. In the emergency room, we had to stay until she was discharged or admitted to the hospital. It's hard to suppress selfish feelings of wanting to be somewhere else. I was sleepy and anxious; I wanted to get out of there as fast as possible. If you are ever having these feelings, realize they are normal and okay.

These feelings are hard to admit because I know this was about Toni. I realize it was even harder on her, yet I couldn't help thinking that the chair I was trying to sleep in was uncomfortable. The TV didn't have the channels I was accustomed to watching. The food was overpriced, and the vending machines didn't have good choices. I tried to resist this, but I could only sit in an uncomfortable chair playing that online game of pool or solitaire for so long. I could only watch so many YouTube videos. These are selfish thoughts that I wish I never had. Still, I had them, and I had them more than once.

I know these feelings sound very bad. I also know, however, that they are an important and unavoidable part of the caregiving reality. There are joys and stressors in caring for a loved one, and this is a stressor. We're all human even though we try to give our all and keep our spirits high. The challenges of the day and the disease weigh heavily.

You may be dealing with the same struggle. Sometimes the selfish feelings don't go away even when you want them to. At those times, you have to think positive thoughts, especially if you are in the process of waiting or even of giving care. Many, if not most, people who have filled the caregiver role have experienced these feelings. Only someone who has been there, in the moment, can relate to this.

However, I caution you that this must be followed by a moment, an hour, or a day when the ONLY thing you care about is YOU. I'm talking about giving your body or mind the permission to shut down. You need to take time strictly for yourself. It's okay to go on vacation or even sleep all day.

There must be these times so you can regenerate and return to caregiving with a big heart, a clear mind, and a fresh approach to the day. My family found this out the hard way. There were several times when we were just exhausted and couldn't get out of our houses to provide care—times when we faced the inability to move at all.

Allowing yourself to be selfish at times can reduce the possibility that there will be any bitterness or resentment on your part. If

I had not gone through the caregiving experience with Toni, I would agree with many who say you should schedule one day a week to do something other than caregiving. The thought process is that patience and motivation are improved by the perspectives that come from taking a break.

I found the best way for me was to give as much care as I could for as long as I could. And then, when I was exhausted or really need a break, I would stop and rest. Trying to schedule something, only to have the appointment broken by an emergency or other immediate need, left me feeling more frustrated and stressed.

Part of giving care is being in the moment. Getting rest when your mind and body need it is what I consider being in the moment. There's not as much guilt or reservation because you won't have the strength to have those feelings. After we had worked ourselves to exhaustion, we allowed ourselves to rest, knowing we had focused all our collective energy on Toni. In this way, we felt justified to take time for ourselves.

Sometimes you will think about a time when caregiving might end. The thought is usually about the possibility that the patient will get better; or it can be about the patient's death. These thoughts are natural and painful. They are normal feelings, and you should indulge them when they come. Allow yourself to have these thoughts even though they come with sadness and pain. They can help you put perspective on your situation.

Whatever you do, it's always good to get professional advice or help when you can. In a lot of cases people have so much stress they can't think clearly. Having a professional who can help you think through issues is a real benefit.

# *Final Thoughts*

As I close my story, I want to offer some advice to anyone who is going through this caregiving journey, or to anyone who might find themselves in this unfortunate situation in the future. In either case, chances are you won't be providing care on your own; you will be doing it with one or more people.

The best way to be effective is to get everyone to agree on shared values, interests, and responsibilities. Make sure each person involved wants the same valuable outcome on which you are focusing, that each shares an interest in the decided course of action, and that each is committed to the specific responsibilities they are given or agree to.

As long as you take this journey as a team with everyone heading in the same direction, you can conquer any challenges. The mental and physical support you will get makes every day a little easier.

Next, I want to tell you that Toni delivered the greatest gift of all before she went to join God—a show of personal strength. The strength she demonstrated throughout her ordeal was amazing, and it gave us strength. What she went through, and how she handled it, made it impossible for me to feel sorry for myself in terms of what I was experiencing by helping Toni battle MS. She showed me the true meaning of strength.

She was strong and committed, and it nurtured her until she went to the Lord. Toni persevered until her son graduated from high school. She raised him mostly on her own through the pain and challenges. He was, and is, the light of her life, and he fought to make sure no one took advantage of her. He stood before people much older and said, "You will not do that," or "You will not say that," or "You will not go there," or "You will not be in that place." He did all of this to support his mom.

Toni is survived by a brother and a sister who put their lives aside to take care of her. They didn't hesitate for one second. Her mother and I laid our resources on the table to take care of her. All of her family members made a sacrifice. Bu no one's sacrifice was greater than Toni's.

Today, Toni's son is working, going to school, and growing into a man very well. Toni's brother is working and preparing to move into a new place after giving up the rental home he shared with his sister. He lives on with the memory of Toni's last moments when he was the only one in the room. Toni's sister continued to manage finances and death notices, and now endures her recovery with her military husband. Toni's mother and I work every day to remember and celebrate Toni, and to give even more love to our surviving children and our grandson. Life moves on, sometimes in slow motion.

Now, my heart is warm with the thought of how Toni touched those around her. The loss of Toni hurts deeply, but there is joy at the same time. She did some remarkable things during those 18 years she endured MS. Toni grew up as a fearless mom, all-star softball player, and cheerleading coach. That strength carried her as far as she could go.

Everyone liked Toni. Even after she got sick and MS started to attack her body and work on her nervous system, she continued to make things happen. She got an associate's degree, she was a fast-food restaurant manager, and she continued to live with and raise her son. Toni purchased a new car and worked a regular job for a very long time—all of it after she was diagnosed with MS. In her last months on this earth, she was still working on more recovery ideas.

At the end, she was so very tired. And she was in pain; we just don't know how much.

I dedicate this poem to my lovely daughter, Toni. May she rest in peace.

# Gone

And now she's gone.
No more hurting.
No more pain.
She is at peace.

Pain is now mine and mine alone.
But when I close my eyes,
She comes to me,
And kisses me,
And tells me I will be fine.

Now I am at peace.

## *About the Author*

Anthony Browne has written on topics such as individual performance, social media, face-to-face communication, emotional intelligence, and leadership.

He served in the military for more than 20 years, and now works for the Department of Defense delivering public relations advice and guidance with the knowledge gained in 40-plus years of military and civilian experience.

This work is his most challenging yet, as it allows him to tell a dynamic story about his daughter.

www.ingramcontent.com/pod-product-compliance
Lightning Source LLC
Chambersburg PA
CBHW071737080526
44588CB00013B/2070